# Bowing Studies

# on Arpeggios

for the cello

book one

by Cassia Harvey

CHP222

©2011 by C. Harvey Publications  All Rights Reserved.

6403 N. 6th Street
Philadelphia, PA 19126
www.charveypublications.com

# String Crossing

**Cassia Harvey**

# 2

## String Crossing and Spiccato

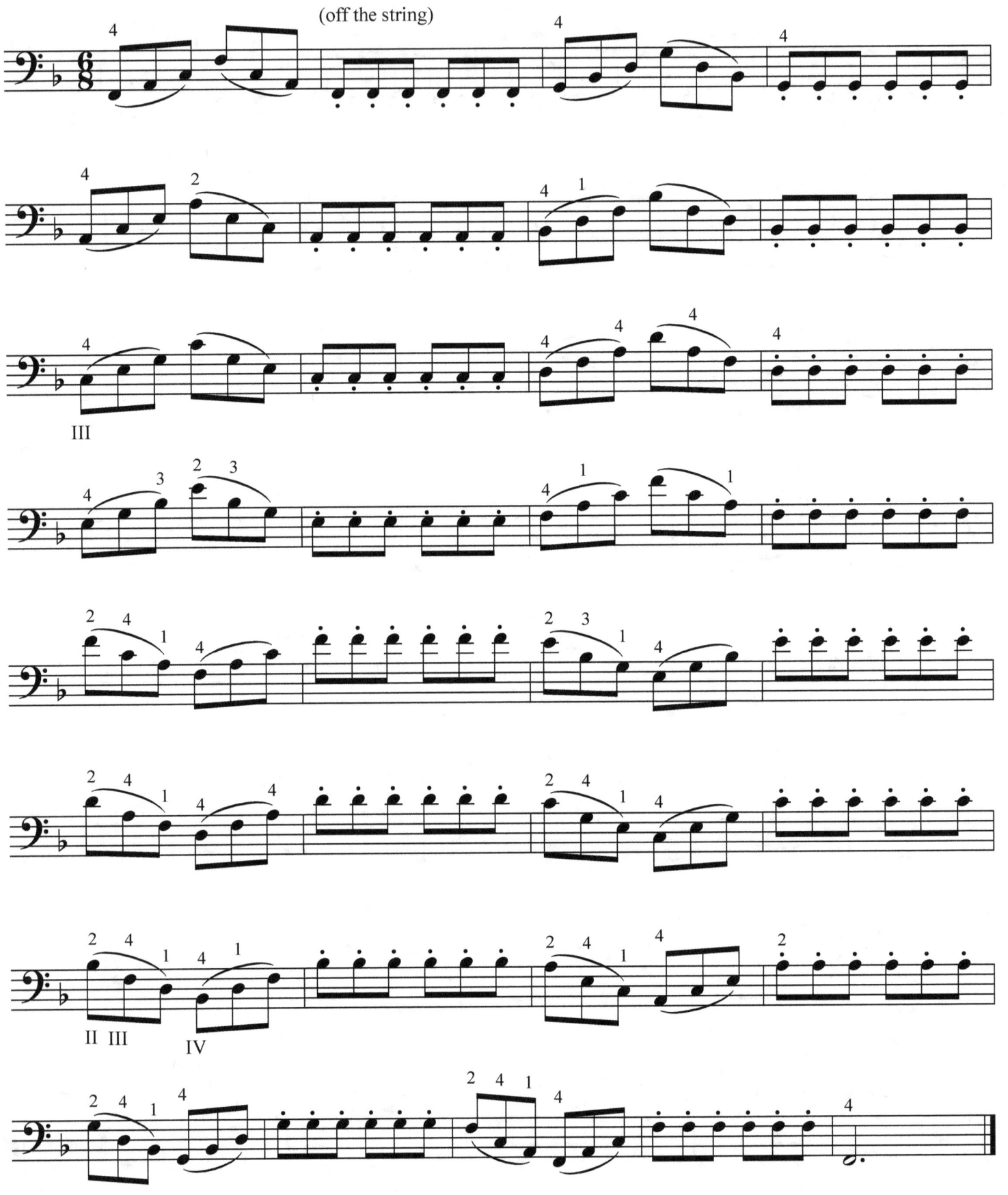

# 3

## String Crossing

# 4
## String Crossing and Spiccato

# 5
## String Crossing and Spiccato

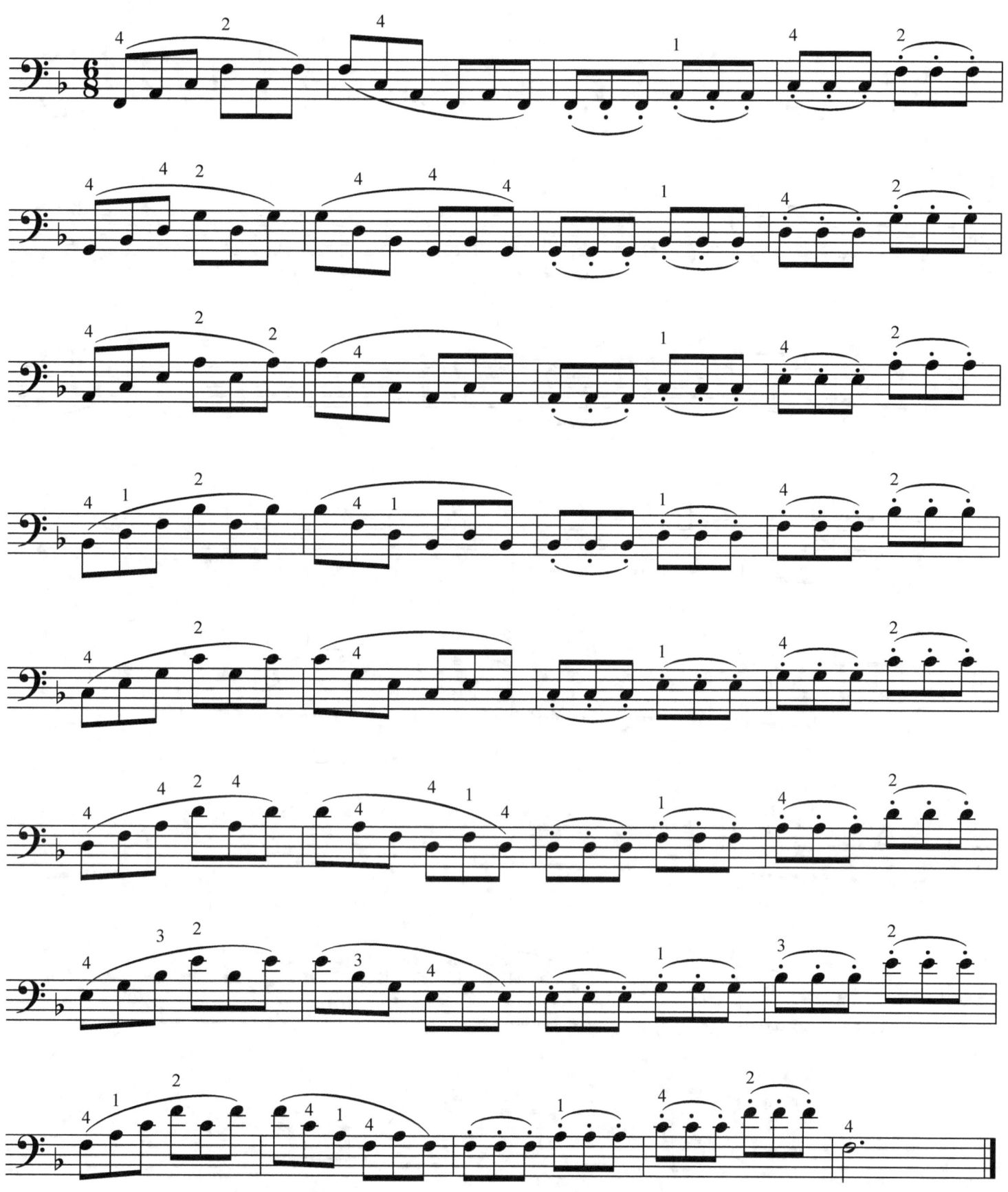

## 6

### String Crossing and Spiccato

# 7

Spiccato; off the string

# 8

Spiccato

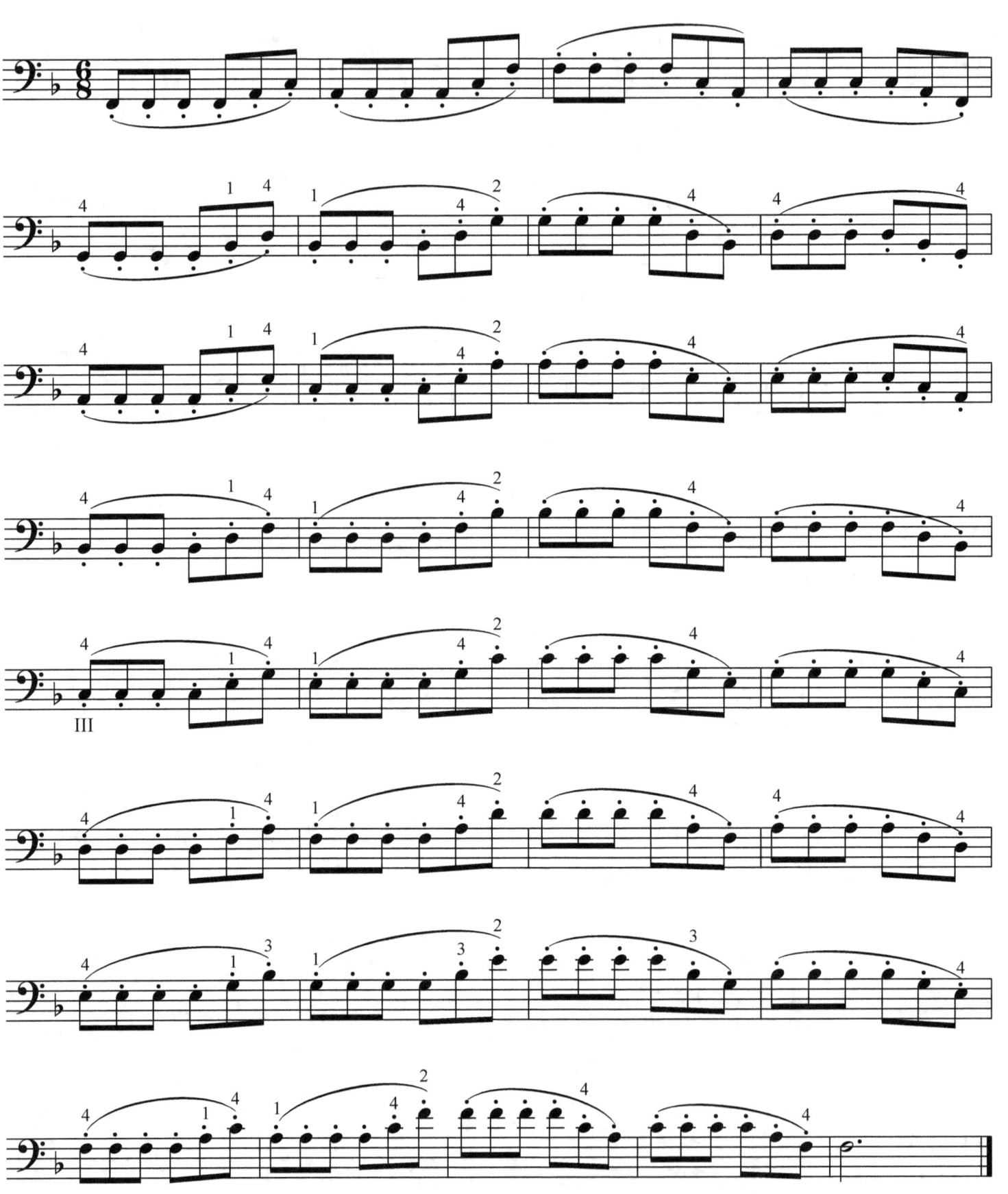

# 9

**Spiccato**

# 10

**Spiccato**

# 11

**Spiccato**

# 12

**Spiccato**

# 13

**Spiccato**

# 14

**Staccato; on the string**

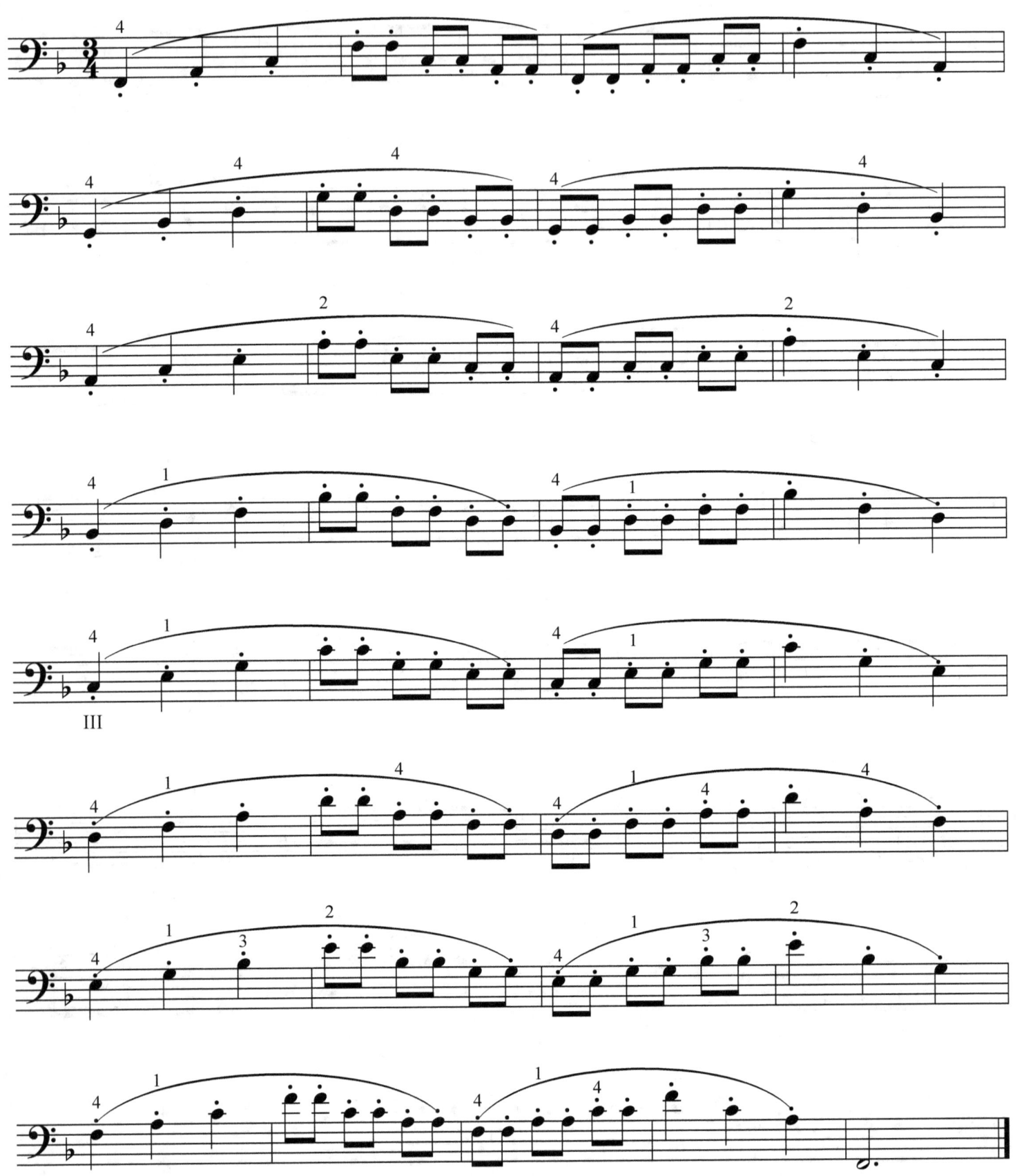

# 15

Staccato

# 16

## String Crossing and Staccato

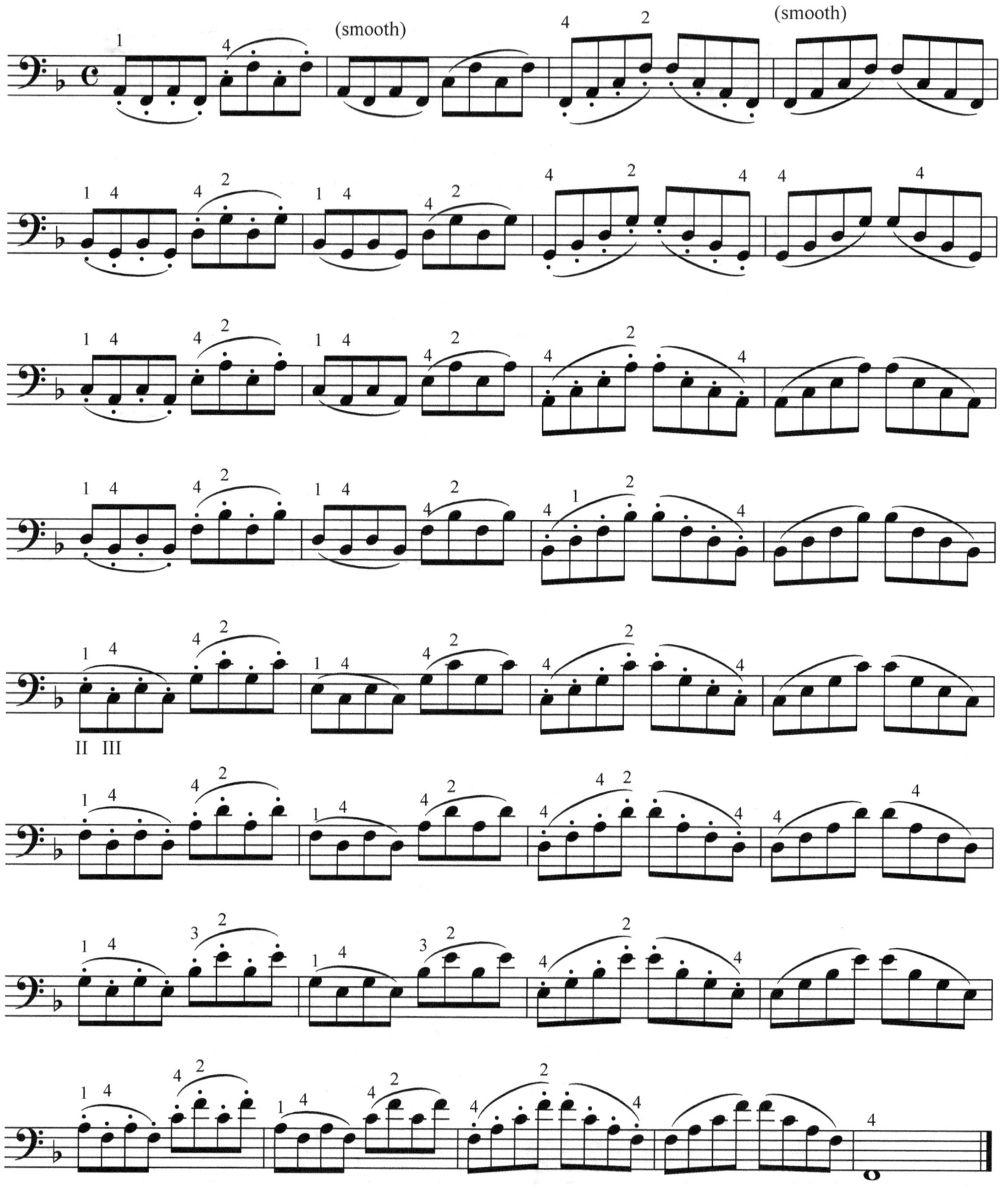

# 17

## String Crossing and Staccato

# 18

## String Crossing and Staccato

# 19

**Staccato**

## 20

**String Crossing and Sautillé**

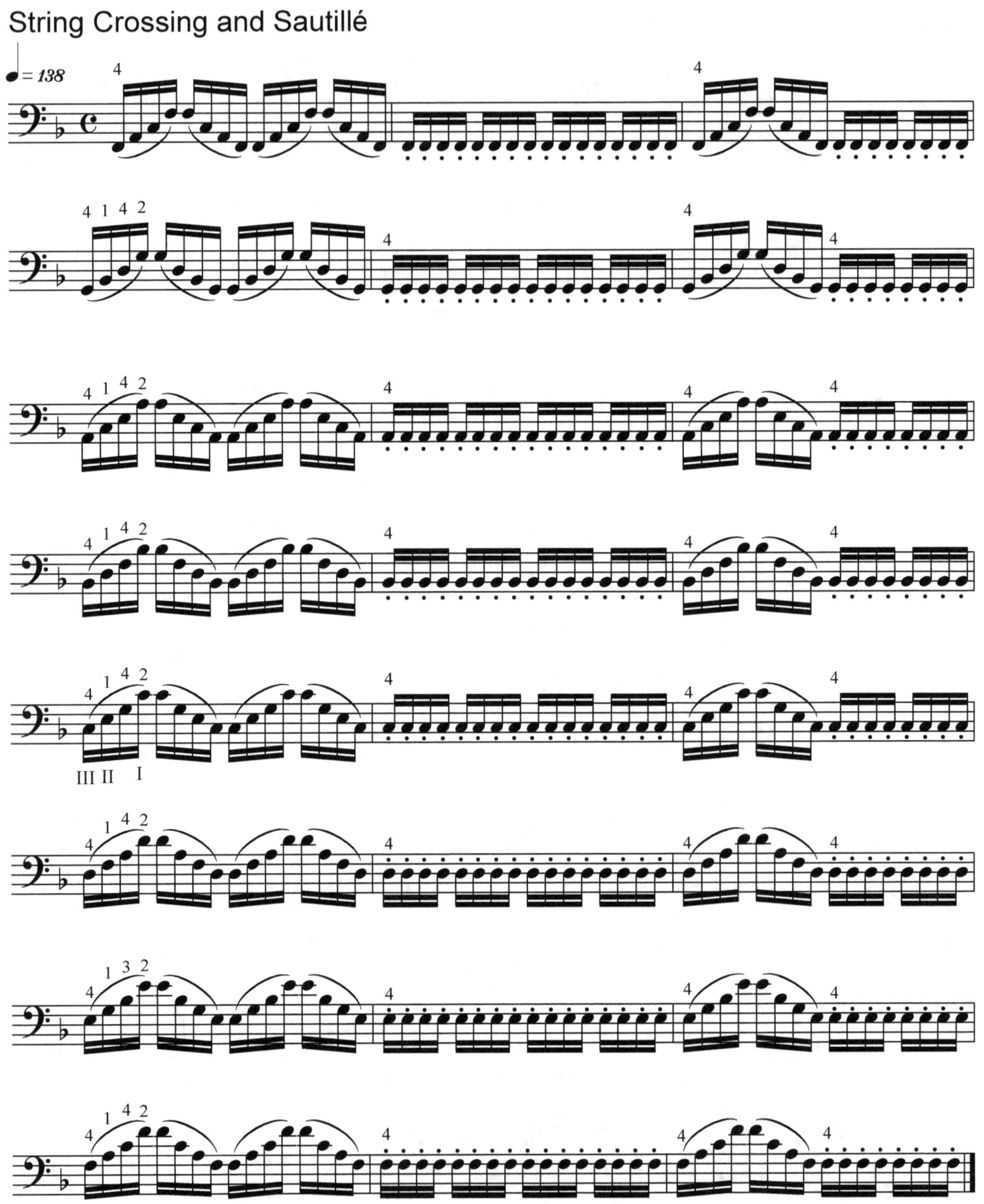

# 21

## String Crossing and Sautillé

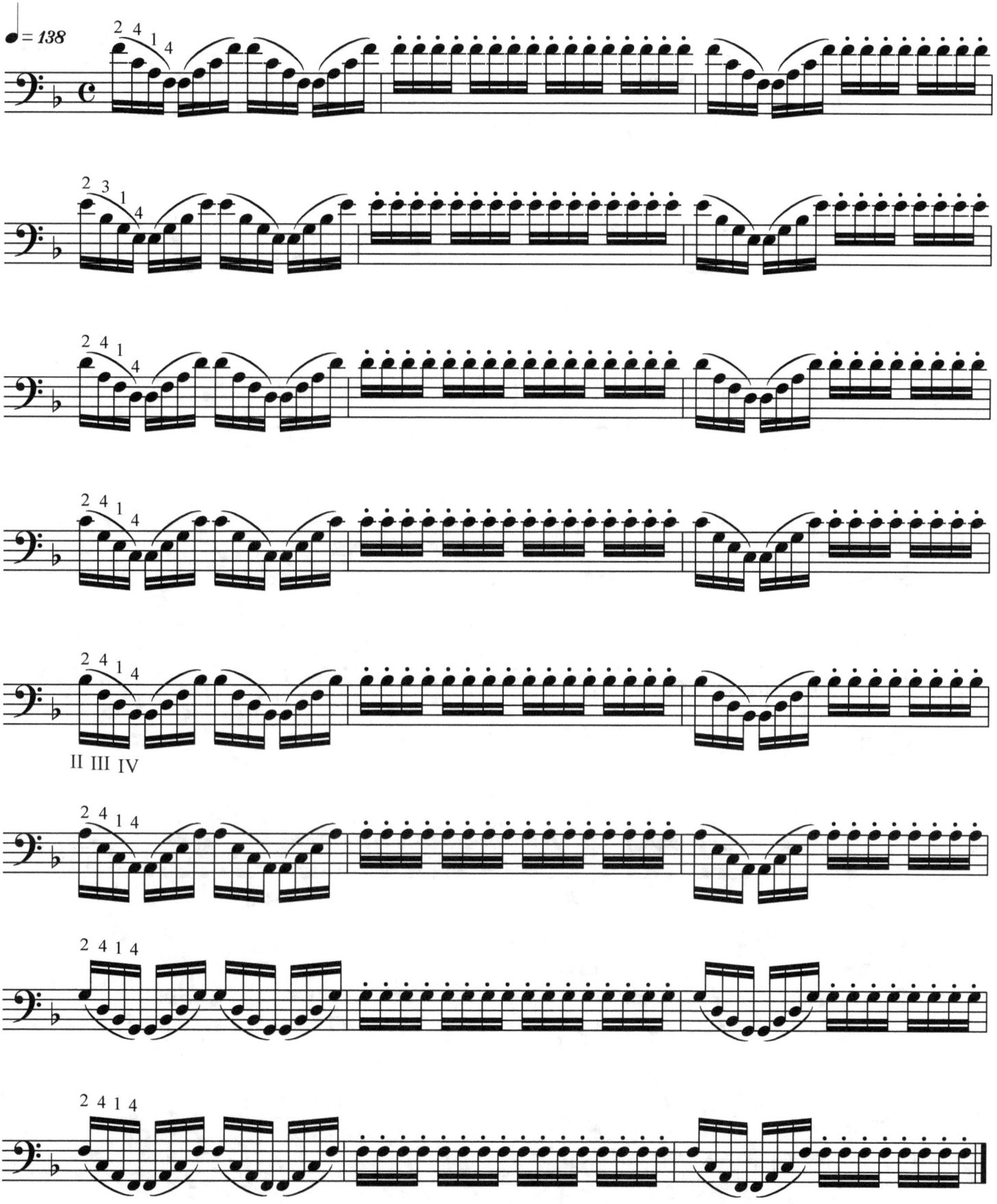

# 22

**String Crossing and Sautillé**

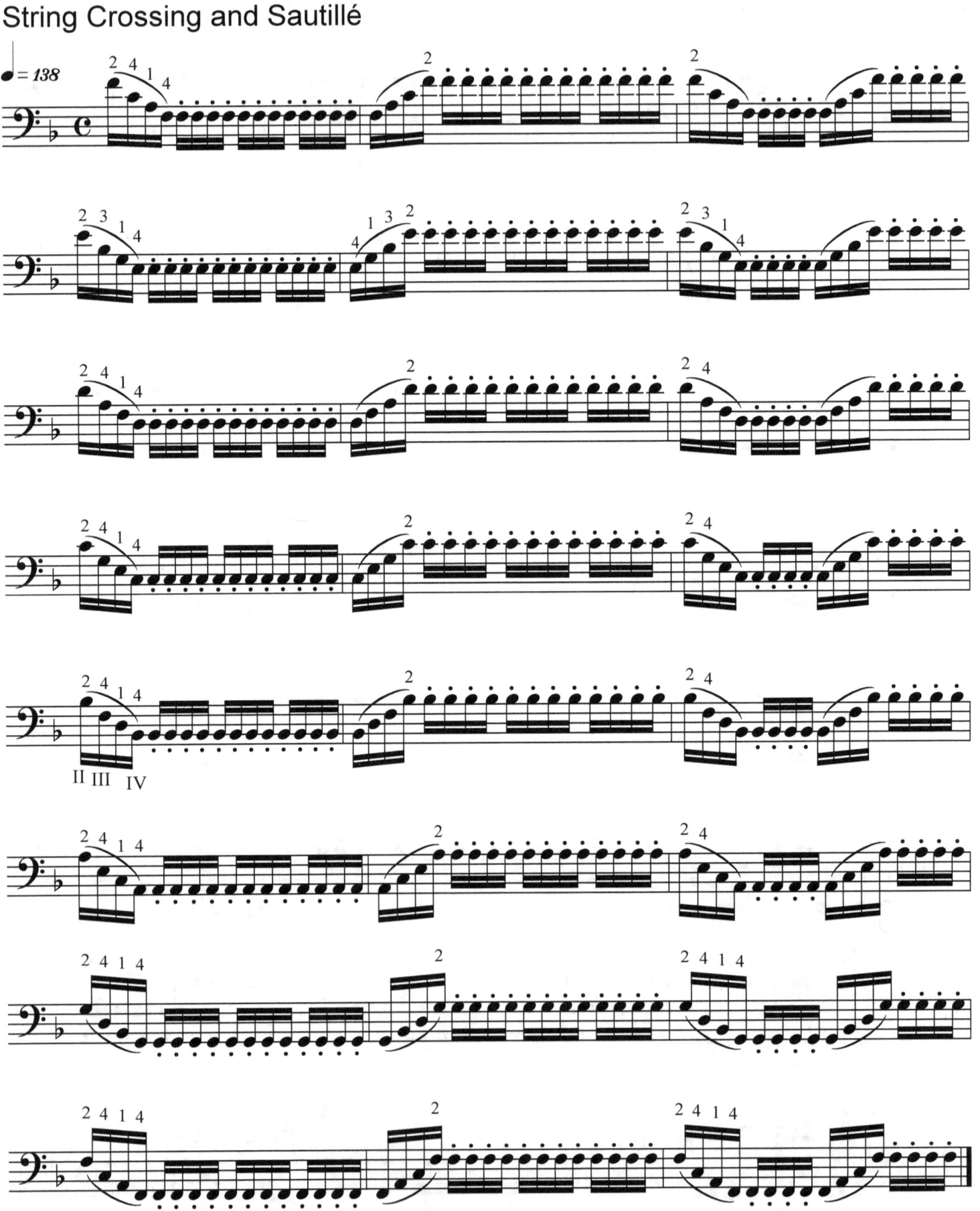

# 23

**String Crossing and Sautillé**

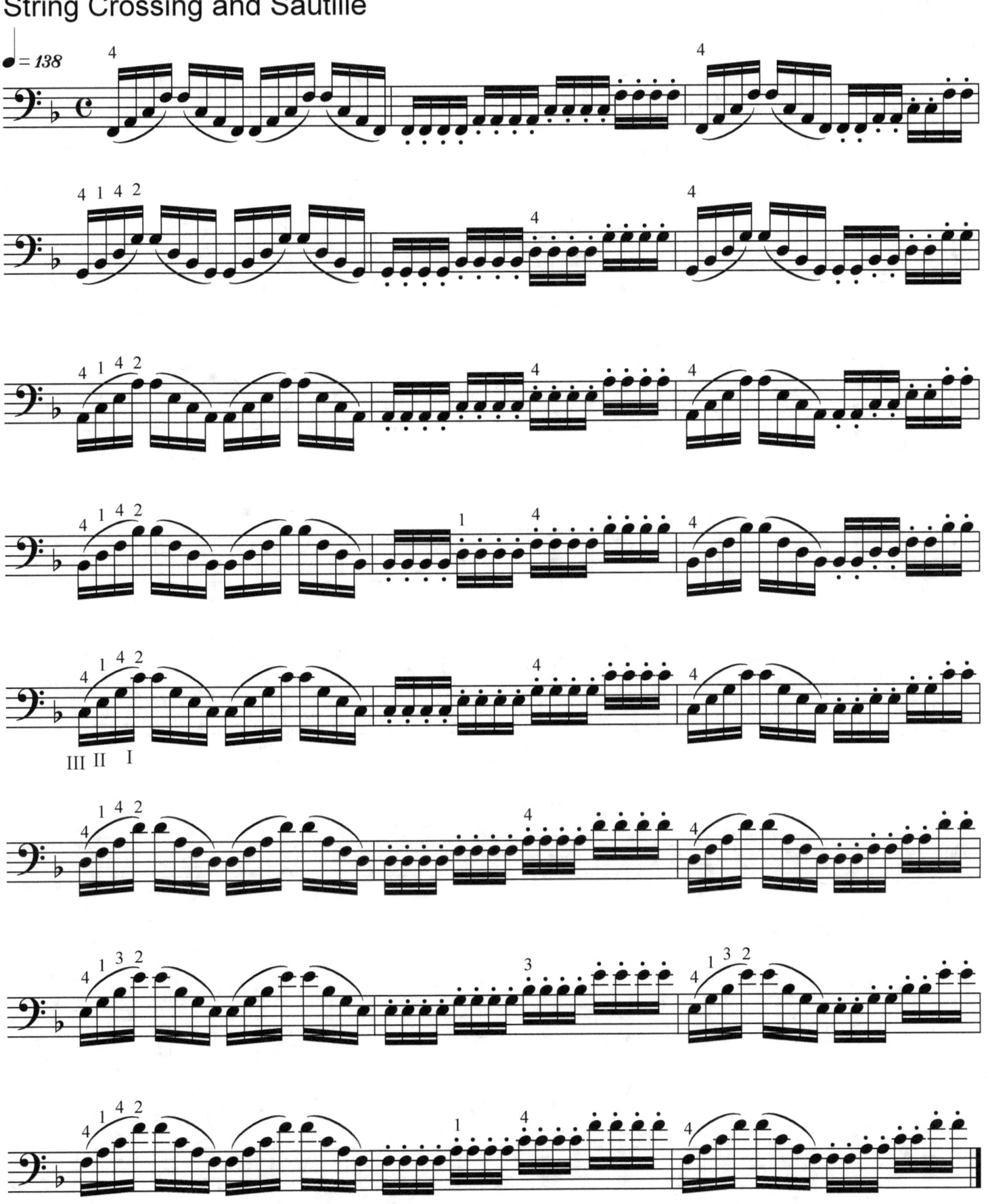

# 24

**Bow Training for Agility**

# 25

## Spiccato and Staccato

# 26

**Skipping Strings**

# Bowing Studies on Arpeggios, for the Cello, Book One

## 27
### String Crossing and String Skipping

# 28

## Bow Training for Agility

# 29
## Bow Training for Agility

# 30

## Bow Training for Agility

# 31

**String Crossing**

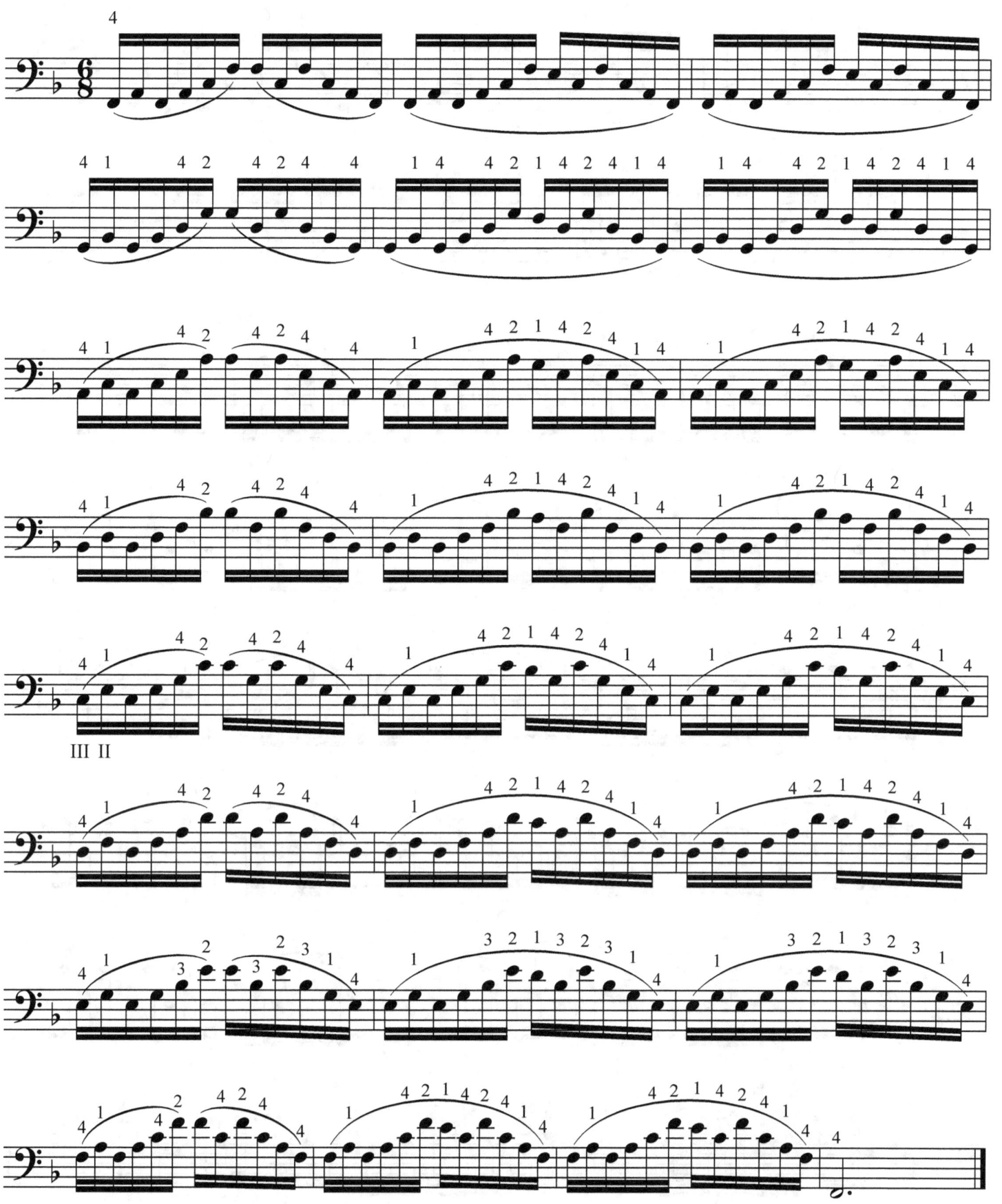

## 32

**String Crossing**

Bowing Studies on Arpeggios, for the Cello, Book One

# 33

Fast Spiccato

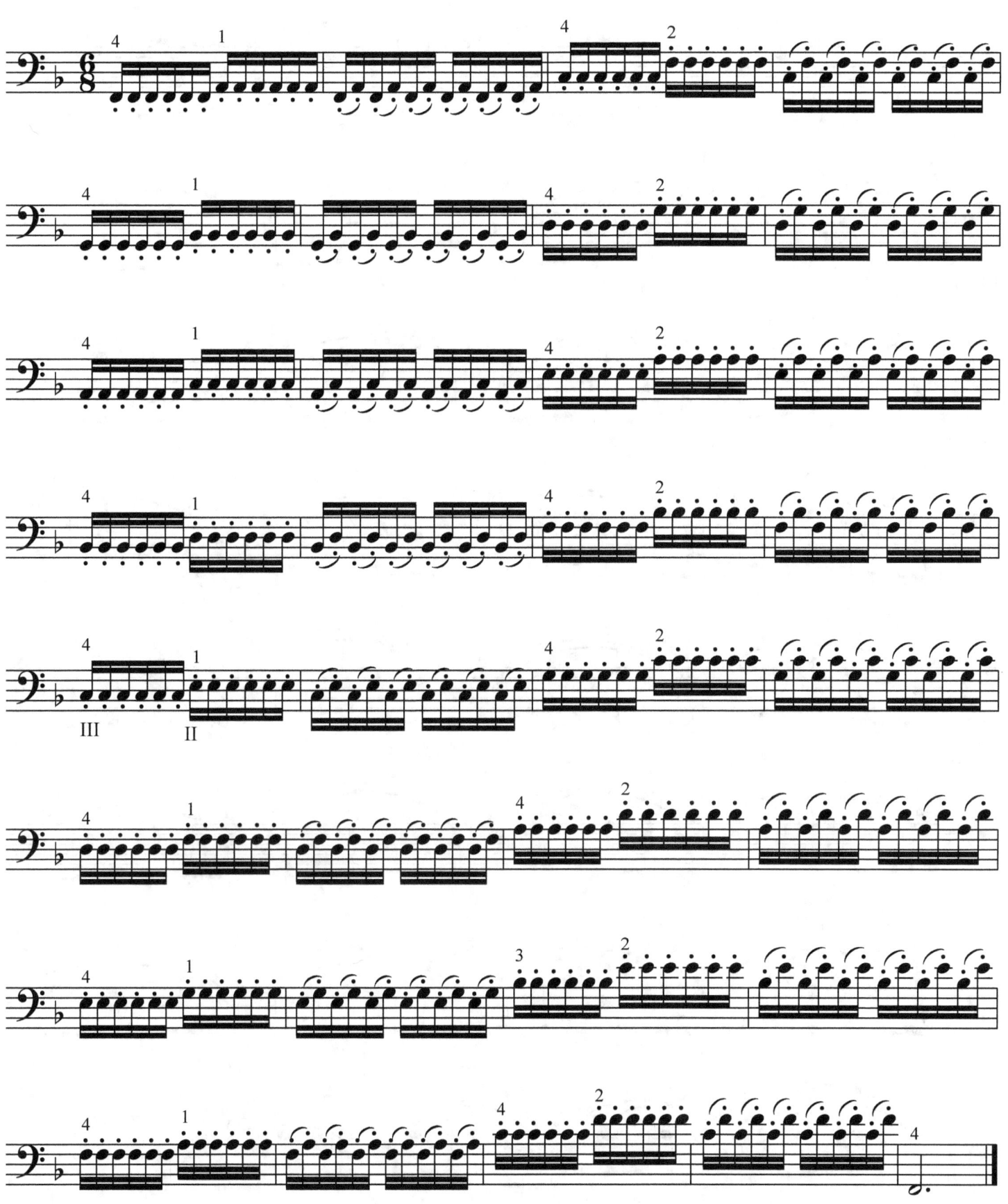

©2011 C. Harvey Publications All Rights Reserved

# 34

**Hooked Bowing**

# 35

**Hooked Bowing**

# 36

**Hooked Bowing**

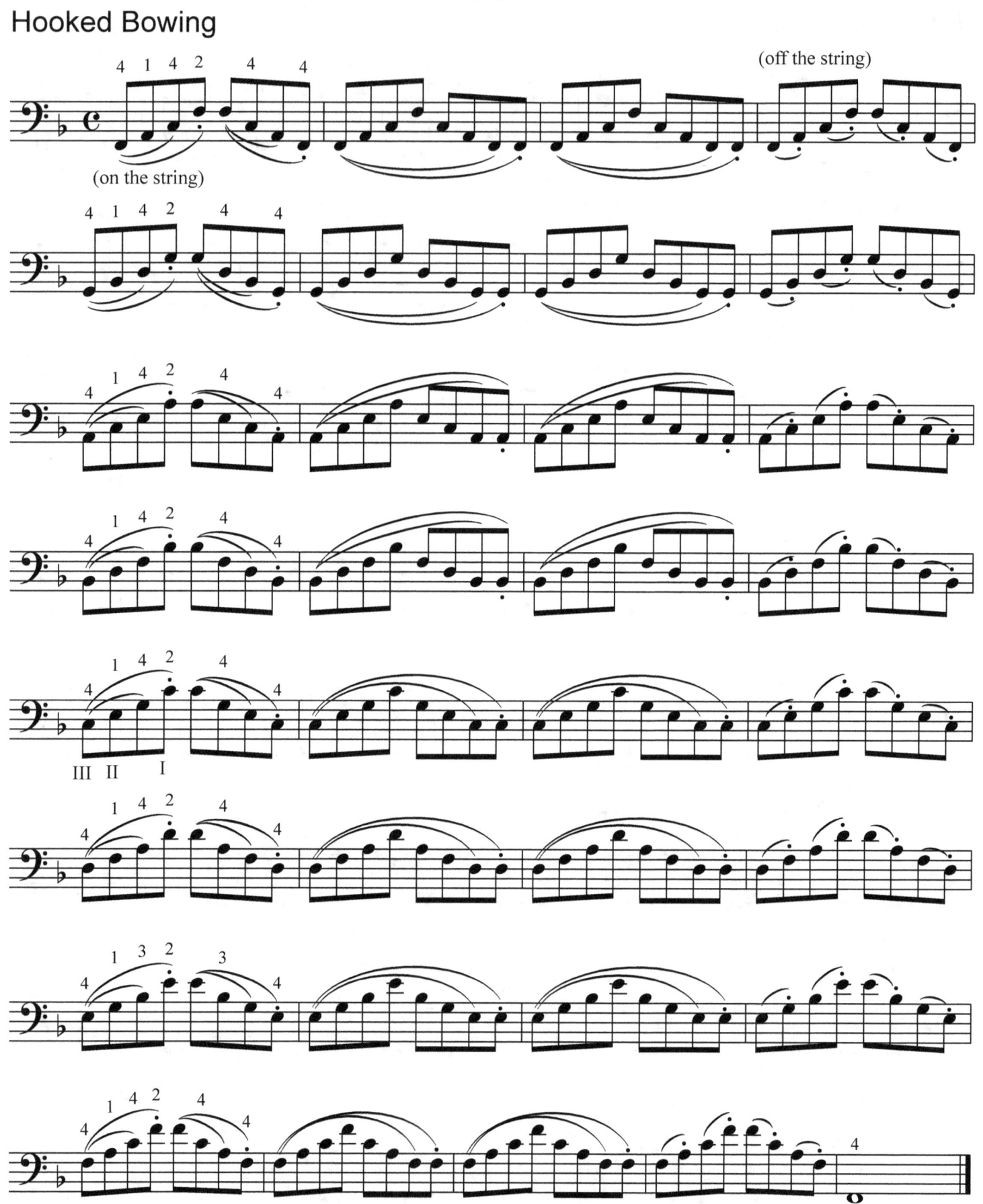

# 37

## Hooked Bowing

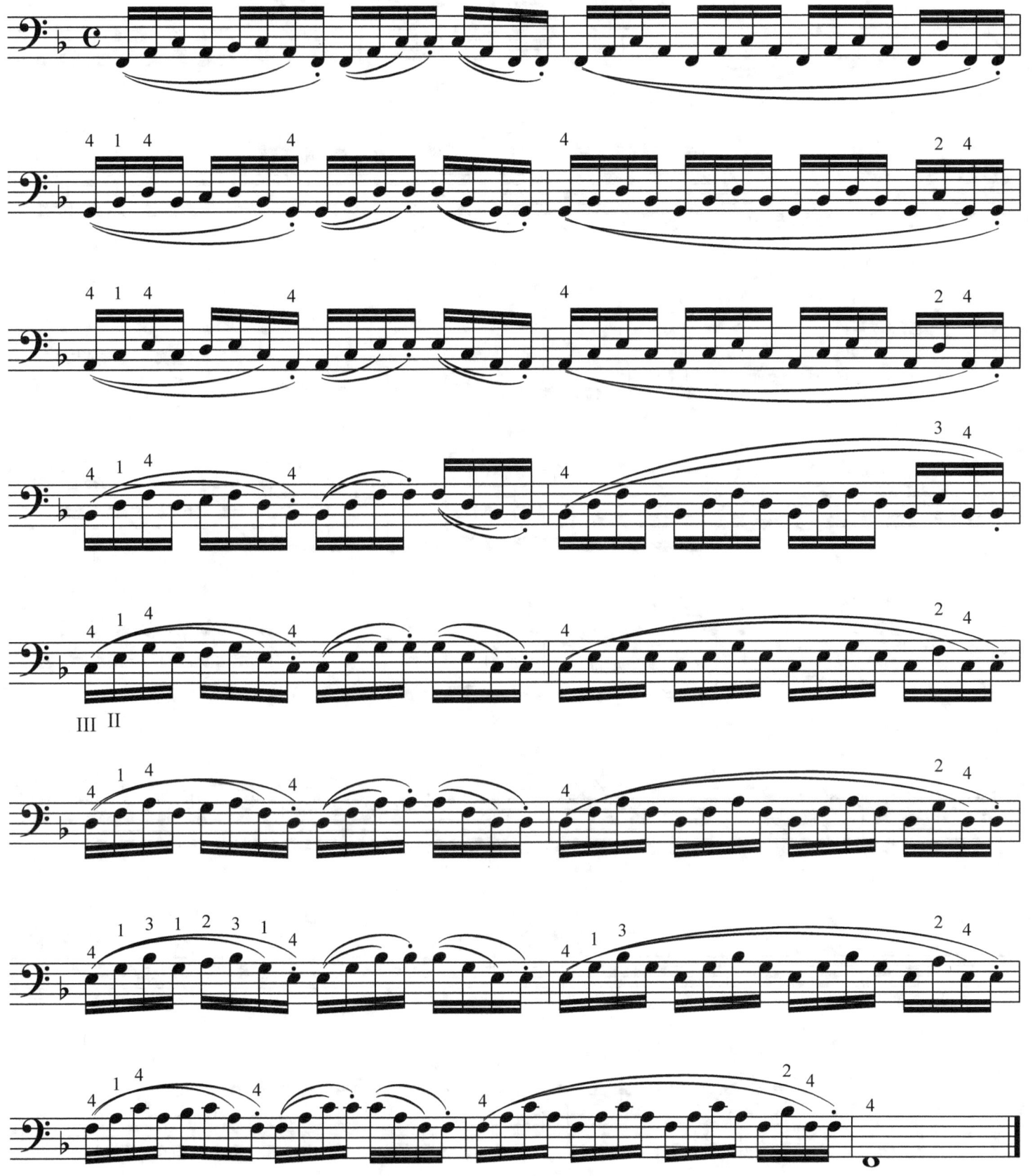

# 38

**Combinations; off the string**

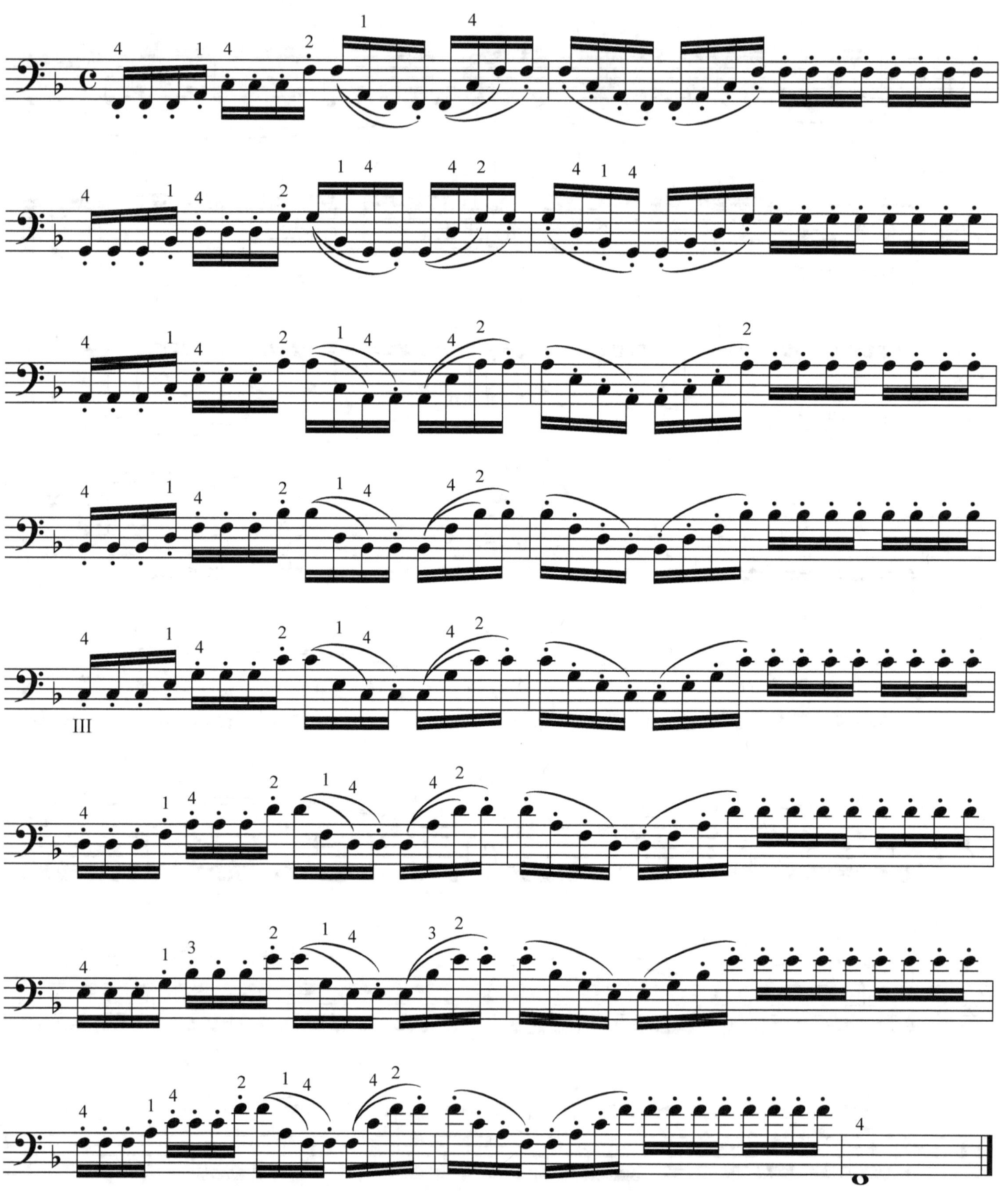

# Bowing Studies on Arpeggios, for the Cello, Book One

## "Springing" bowing

### 39

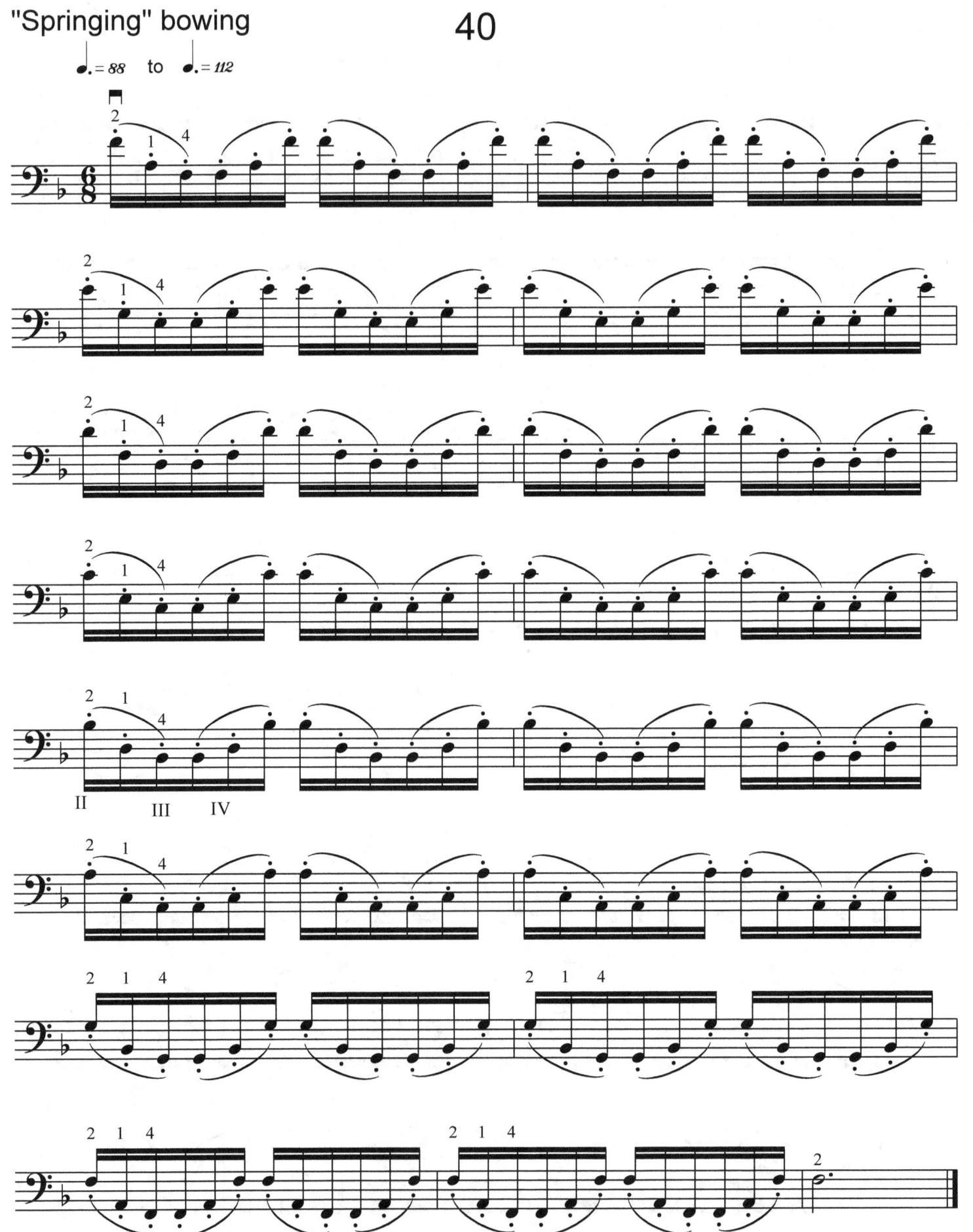

Bowing Studies on Arpeggios, for the Cello, Book One

# 41

Ricochet

# 42

Ricochet

Bowing Studies on Arpeggios, for the Cello, Book One

# 43

**Ricochet**

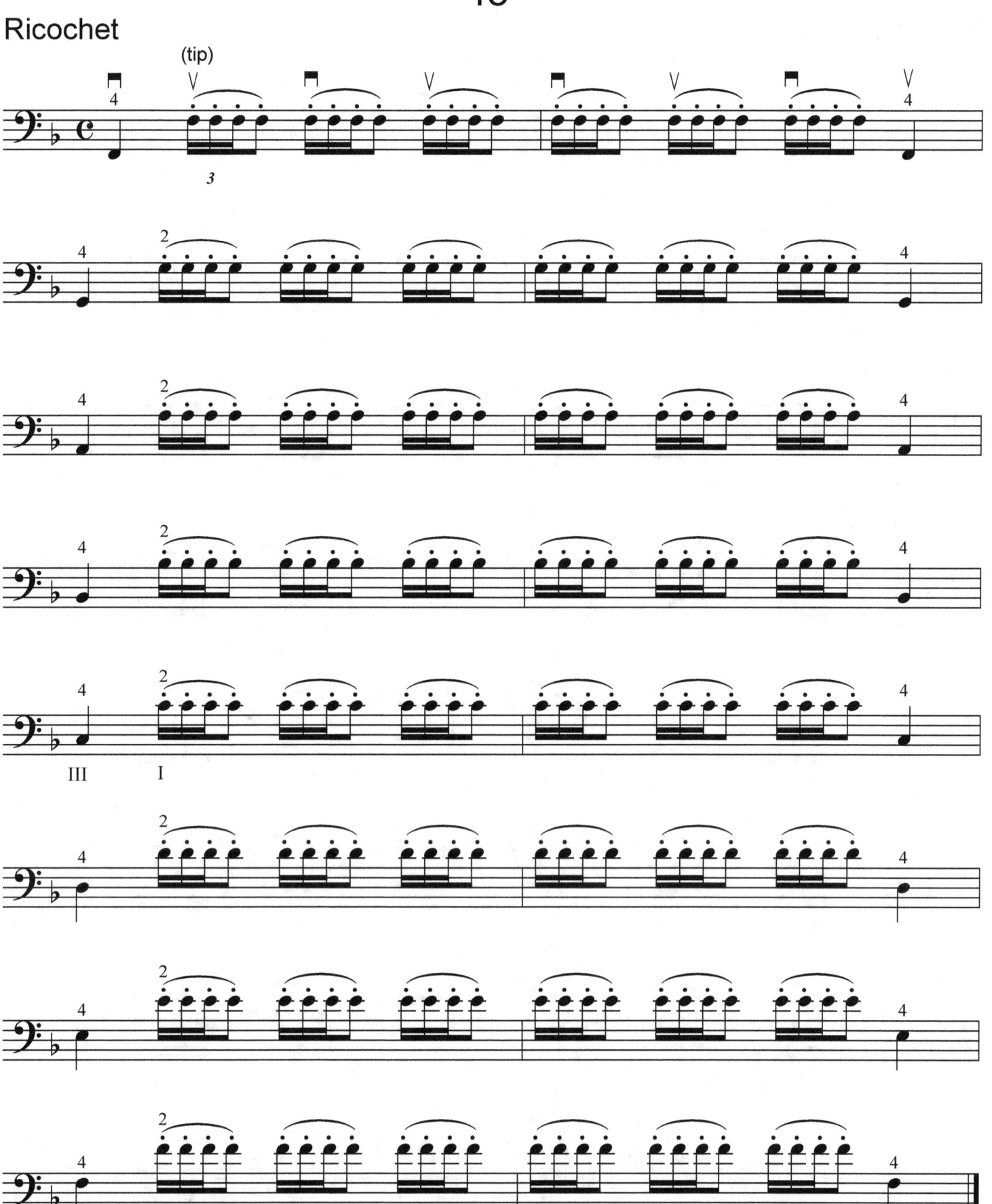

## 44

**Ricochet**

# 45

**Ricochet**

# available from www.charveypublications.com: CHP332
## The Bach Cello Suite No. 1 Study Book

Note: The Suite is broken up into sections in this study book. The complete Suite is at the back of the book.

### Suite No. 1: Prelude
Part One: Measures 1-4 (Bowing #1)

Suite by J. S. Bach
Exercises by Cassia Harvey

### Double Stops for Intonation
Measures 1-4

©2017 C. Harvey Publications All Rights Reserved.

www.ingramcontent.com/pod-product-compliance
Lightning Source LLC
Chambersburg PA
CBHW051425070526
44584CB00023B/3590